Breakfast at Denny's

Breakfast at Denny's

Jill

I had a couple of these books
left over from a reading and signing I
did several years ago. They were part
of a first, limited press, release before the
book actually came out — in case I became
famous. Hahaha

Jim

Jim McGarrah

INK
BRUSH
PRESS

Limited Pre-release Edition
This copy is # ____ of 100

INK
BRUSH
PRESS

ISBN: 978-0-9839715-8-0

Library of Congress Control Number: 2012952182

Manufactured in the United States

Ink Brush Press

Temple and Dallas, Texas

Acknowledgements

Thanks to Amy Leighty, Matthew Graham, Shawna K. Rodenberg, and Ron Mitchell for editorial advice and encouragement.

The author gratefully acknowledges the first publication of some of the poems in this volume by the following journals and anthologies:

Agave, Avatar Review, Blast Furnace Magazine, Café Review Cincinnati Review, DuPage Valley Review, Future Cycles Press, GreenBriar Review, North American Review, Open 24 Hours, Spectrum Magazine, Winning Writers

Poetry from Ink Brush Press

Alan Birkelbach and Karla Morton, *No End of Vision: Texas as Seen by Two Laureates*

Jerry Bradley, *The Importance of Elsewhere*

Millard Dunn, *Places We Could Never Find Alone*

Chris Ellery, *The Big Mosque of Mercy*

Charles Inge, *Brazos View*

McGehee, Pittman, *Growing Down*

Steven Schroeder, *a dim sum of the day before*

Steven Schroeder and Sou Vai Keng, *a guest giving way like ice melting*

Jan Seale, *Nape*

Jan Seale, *The Wonder Is*

W.K. Stratton. *Dreaming Sam Peckinpah*

Chuck Taylor, *At the Heart*

Jesse Waters, *Human Resources*

For information on these and other Ink Brush Press books go to
www.inkbrushpress.com

This book is dedicated to the memory of Jack Myers who taught me to break no rules unless I knew what the rules were and then there were no rules.

My Irish Heritage

My ancestors proved how easily
the process of living becomes death.

They wore knitted wool sweaters,
thousands of threads stitched into maps
so strangers who found these warrior poets

lying still on ancient battlefields
might carry them home to rest.

Contents

We Need a Man for My Wife Carrie. We Will Drive to You. Call 867-593-9192.

—Sign on a restroom wall in a Texaco Station outside Macon, Georgia, circa 1969

We Sit Here Stranded Though We All Do Our Best to Deny It

In War There Are no Unwounded Soldiers

I roll on a wave and look at white clouds

Epilogue

We Need a Man for My Wife Carrie. We Will Drive to You. Call 867-593-9192.

—Sign on a restroom wall in a Texaco Station outside

Macon, Georgia, circa 1969

Interstate 24

I'm forty-nine miles from Chattanooga

stumbling through the radio in my pick-up truck

searching for noise to take away the ceaseless buzz

of tread bare Goodyear tires. Like a shark,

inertia drives me crazy. I decide a burred bearing

sounds better than Michael Buble & settle on a female

preacher who whines, "Beer is the real problem"

& I think of Jesus, his blanched bones scattered,

his soul in a make believe place, flesh desiccated

so our apathy matters. Jesus—wanting

only a draft or two of Pabst Blue after a hard day

with hammer & nails & blisters trying to carpenter

something solid, yet knowing nothing

of how to build paradise. Then, cousin John

coaxes him to a stream, holds his head under water,

deprives his brain of air till god appears as a dove.

That's when Jesus ends up hung on a stake, a carcass

of transubstantiation so the rest of us can feed on his misery

with our Inquisitions & Crusades, jihads & dead Jews,

televangelists who love meth & priests who love little boys.

Hell, we can't get ourselves born without originally sinning.

Then, a revelation comes in a blinding flash of lights

from a semi in the wrong lane, kinda like that time

when old apostle Paul fell off his mule on the road to Damascus. Bang! This radio lady's bat-shit crazy and, no sister, beer ain't the *real* problem.

Collateral Damage

Marge leans against air.
It's the one solid object in her life.
She rides to a hospice and reads
the news each day to her vegetative son—
his face unchanged through her litanies
of genocides, fratricides, riptides, and pedophilia.
"We're all collateral damage in God's design,"
she says at least twice a week. "It's the price
we must pay for being human."

We're waiting on the 19,
a new eco-friendly bio-diesel bus
the mayor claims will reduce carbon footprints.
It's late this morning and a plump school girl
bums a smoke from the plumber whose car
got swallowed by the bank. With his footprint
already gone, he needs a ride to a new job
and she's been banned from the school bus
for terrifying small children with her adolescence.
I search for headlights in the predawn dark,
enduring this street corner, unable to admit
what we all fear, that time lost
is the one way misery gets measured.

For me, god's plan remains elusive,

the cost too high for my faithless budget.

The good seems neither greater nor patterned,

more circumstance than intent. Like roulette

it traps us in some relentless hole where

we bear random wounds in solitary confinement

as the spin of the wheel wears down

and sometimes allow ourselves a state of grace,

as the boy I saw in Bosnia playing basketball

on one leg, the other blended with the scree

of a minefield where he attended school once,

or as these people waiting at this bus stop

who suffer silently the ache of unearned despair.

Parallax View

Tonight, I drink enough tequila
that when I change barstools
without falling, the barmaid laughs.
She knows my short trip home
will bring applause from neighbors
who wonder what new existential
crisis drove me into this stupor.
I will entertain, but not confess,
the notion that my silence
protects them all from wisdom,
a thing so profound its existence
shifts perspective in direct proportion
to my consumption. For example,
I am certain that the Cuervo bottle
slipped its label after my fourth shot
and now reads Don Julio Blanco.
Is it a taste thing? No. It's a miracle,
like Nietzsche resurrected as Jesus,
like discovering the car next to mine
isn't the one moving as I drive away.
Suffering these astute breakthroughs,
or parallax views, the way some do arthritis
brings me relief from the pain of thought

rubbing thought in my brain during

the process unwise people call life.

Driving by My Childhood Home Forty Years Later

The paint peels now and the magnolia tree,

sawn to stump, is pedestal for a birdbath,

foundation for a trellis of honeysuckle vines.

From the door on the west corner, my room opened

outward once till nailed shut, a father's failed effort

to keep his young son from self-destructive wanderlust.

The pear tree withers, the neighbors have died,

and I'd like to look inside, view the rooms

where grandma came to live and nanny us

when Mom joined the workforce so we could buy

our first color TV. Grandma used to prop sis and me

on her goose down mattress, warm beneath the quilts,

while she knitted sweaters slowly and tried to ignore

the chill that came from knowing even time has its limits.

On Saturdays, we'd watch Buffalo Bob Barker

pull Howdy Doody's puppet strings on Channel Six,

thankful school was out and waiting as the neighborhood

came alive soon with Schwinn bikes, hula hoops,

and the weekly whiffle ball game. Not one of us ever

knew a drive-by shooting or the collapse of world finance.

The fear of being trapped by boredom drove us crazy.

It festered in our guts till

this curdled milk of small town ennui—the idea

that happiness is always somewhere else—steered us

separate ways to larger cities and more exotic dreams,

to seek the lives we left before our deaths arrive.

On the Streets of Saigon in the 21st Century After Reading a U.S. Court Decision Finding the Makers of Agent Orange Not Responsible For Birth Defects in Vietnamese Children

They swarmed me like hummingbirds

a flock of boys two generations from war

twitching so fast in the white sun I hardly saw

the animated hunger hiding in their dark eyes.

With watches and postcards held aloft,

some scuttled on skateboards while others

scraped kneepads and bike gloves

along Dong Khoi Street dragging knapsacks

full of salvaged treasure, Zippos, rings,

bullet jacket brass, photos, and private things

torn from battle dead thirty years before

these casualties were ever born.

Their humid voices echoed over traffic

and claxtons from cargo ships, some moored,

others dry-docked in the Bason shipyard.

I bought a pack of 555's from tiny twins,

maybe twelve years old, maybe fifty.

The acrid smoke veiled the stench of dead

fish rising from the Saigon River as the whole

group hailed a cyclo driver for my ride to peace,
my reason for return, a ceremony by the Ministry
of Arts and Literature, an invitation to remember,
a celebration of repentance and forgiveness.
Each child waved goodbye as if we were cousins,
ordinary people with ordinary lives.
Some used their only hand, those without arms
shook their feet, three wriggled fingers attached
to legs, one whose torso was backward turned
away and gave me a hug. The twins, fused
at the ears, smiled a bizarre double grin
born from three chipped and blackened teeth.

A Savage Cup of Coffee

This barista brings out the animal in me. You might think it has to do with the way her nipples stretch the red tee shirt or the precise cross hatching of her braided hair. Sure, her glide between the coffee machine and the pastry case, like a ballerina in sneakers one second and a stripper on a pole the next, flogs my old blood into adolescent frenzy. When she breaks and sits next to me, knees tucked beneath her chin as calyx for the blossom of her face, cinnamon overwhelms the room. But, this is all romantic crap—really. When I admit to savage lust not romance, the owner of this faux-beatnik coffee house full of unread books and strange paintings takes offense at my use of the word "savage" and deems me racist toward Indians—not the kind of Indians who design rocket guidance systems or own all of America's motels, but rather the kind with buckskins and buffalo or feathers and arrows, the Lone Ranger's Tonto kind and HBO's Squanto kind, the Indians that suffer from the detritus of Manifest Destiny. It seems this person grew up on a reservation. You know, one of those sterile, hopeless, desert prisons where we white folk cage the ugly part of our history. Yet, my urge to pluck this innocent—or maybe not so pure—barista from her seat and run my lips across her silken neck until her breathing gets heavy and rapid does not seem to me reserved for red men. My ancestors lived in Ireland before time. With blue painted faces and feral cries they clubbed enemies to death and laughed at the lamentations of their women. I want my own savagery respected.

Elegy for Charles Darwin

(on the 150th Anniversary of *The Origin of Species*
and during the trial of Faith Healer Dale Neuman)

He reasoned we'd evolve,

become greater than the sum of our parts,

but Darwin never met Dale,

who killed his daughter with prayer

because doctors are devils.

He conjectured we'd adapt

from the inside, like Stop Leak,

and plug the holes in our lives,

bar our souls from oozing out,

check ignorance from seeping in.

Darwin surmised we'd adjust

to our futures, but Dale didn't like

this new century full of free will,

science minus magic, and no gods left

to exorcise his daughter's diabetic demons.

Dale prayed, injecting spirit instead

of insulin, and for his faith, his prayers

were answered. A coma cured the child

and sent her back to Jesus, a home where

Darwin's evil is barred from entry.

The Immigrants—1929

Grandpa healed great locomotives, herding them

out of Southern Railway shops along the veins of tracks

connecting both coasts to the Hoosier heartland. Paid enough

for bread and a few of those potatoes the Irish learned to love,

he brought home a bag of coal every week in winter

to fire the iron stove rising from the floor like a black orchid.

That stove split the house into kitchen and parlor.

Grandma bought "blue john" milk from a horse drawn wagon

and enough sugar to make the oatmeal taste better than paste,

but all that luxury ended when the stock market crashed.

The Southern trains quit running. Not afraid of hard labor

Grandpa took odd jobs at first, then hired on the WPA

to clear brush, swing a pick, bust rock into gravel and build

a hundred farm roads that still crisscross Gibson county.

Depression had more to do with cash than self-esteem.

If he plowed no garden no garden got plowed, fed no chickens

no chickens were fed, and dinner wasn't as long on presentation

as it was practicality in those lean days, those days they learned

that living with need was better than giving in or up.

Grandma shared no patience with wastrels in her house.

My dad and uncle "Ding" split wood or went to bed hungry,

although a hobo might sample apple pie if the budget

had allowed for a show of wealth on a particular week.

Rules sustained their home—

Treat others better than you would treat yourself.

If you must steal to keep from going hungry, go hungry.

Curse only when the Cardinals lose the pennant.

Never take a drink on Sunday or use spittoons in the house.

Say nothing at the dinner table that doesn't sound grateful.

Show all women respect and all men equality.

When you die, let no one wish it had happened sooner—

They followed these daily and never knew they were poor.

An Existentialist in Utopia

(in memory of a famous Christian theologian whose memorial is strangely placed behind the Red Geranium Restaurant at New Harmony, Indiana)

Drunk one night, I stumbled

over Paul Tillich's tomb

in these harmonic woods.

A goose empowered by god

to guard three bedraggled tulips

growing from his blanched,

but sacred, grave attacked

my testicles with fowl zeal.

The angry bird chased me

toward a pond that lay

beyond the bronzed monument

erected by a crazed woman

named Jane who, widowed

from the heir to the Owenites,

was willed this tiny town.

Rumor has it she knew Tillich—

his systematic theology, his

socialist agenda, his existential

dread that squawked

at absent gods like this

future Christmas dinner

honks at my family jewels—

in a biblical way.

I heard Jane passed recently

and have no wish

to speak ill of the dead, but I do

wonder who else would have

trained this feathered ninja

to do the lord's work?

It must have been her

fevered hope that somehow

in his heavenly home of dirt

old Paul might rest unmolested,

assured his soul had found

its final meaning.

Appetite

I want to be an urge that comes on
unannounced, unbidden, and uncontrolled,
like the one prompting this woman who
piles her plate with mashed potatoes
smothered in lead-gray gravy at the Pilot
Truck Stop buffet on Highway One
where I drink coffee and wait for fame.

Her hungry forage at the steam table,
her swelling workload for a busboy, loses
neither poise nor lust and makes me wish
someone craved me with this same driving
passion or even a longing strong enough
to save me from Willie Nelson's jukebox
keening and a burnt-toast smell on my waitress.

Popcorn Sutton

Knock-kneed, bent double, twisted
as a coat hanger, hacking from a Lucky
that drips constantly from his lips,
Popcorn still scuttles crab-like around
his copper tubes, weighed down

by no concerns that plague us city folk
to death—mortgage payments, layoffs,
and boredom hanging like a shroud
of smog across any city's shoulders.
He has always known purpose and art.

Both drain from the spigot on his copper kettle
into Mason jars. After forty years, Popcorn
still makes the best whiskey I ever drank.
His truck veers only slightly from the paths
cut through Carolina brush by his father's father.

When corn prices went too high
and demand for untaxed liquor fell below the risk
of its production, when his sons switched
to curing cannabis and cousins sold their land
for housing tracts, Popcorn kept faith in our thirst.

Only the heartless forget heritage

to satisfy greed. At least that's what

he told me on my last trip south

and I respect a man who writes his own story

without regard for market value. Think

James Joyce in bib overalls, Pynchon with

a shotgun on his lap, or some barely read poet

the world never knows but is enlarged by each poem.

Underground Inheritance

A cold wind howls through a holler,

kicks the dust from forsaken barns along

that strip of road in Floyd and Carcassone.

It's the same Kentucky air that ate away

the "Mail Pouch" and "See Rock City" signs

on Route 23 when daddy drove us to church

to pray away the holy ghost of four dead miners.

I was twelve and he was forty, dying from

the black lung that now stings my graveled breath.

U. S. Coal owns my town no longer, but coal

owns me because it must be dug by shovel,

by pick, but mostly by blood and bone

'cause it won't free itself by itself

from these ancient hills no more

than I will free myself from the need

to feed my family by my death.

The Garvin Gate Music Festival in Louisville, Kentucky

I

On the corner of Oak and Fourth
townhouses from a bygone era,
rusty red with age and hard use,
face the makeshift wooden bandstand.

In between music makers
and brick walls, the hot street shimmies
with strange revenants of a time
when even Baptists understood

harmony, rhythm and good wine,
not unlike the blood of Jesus,
covered a multitude of sins.
A plumber's shop, a Dollar Store,

the hair salon, and one old whore
stand unused, idled by the blues.

II

There's one in every crowd
listening with his hands, convinced
that life has left him with fingers
to graft his soul into the sound,

grow beyond sums of frequency
and pitch or limits of an ear.
This man, lean and long, clicks two spoons
together on his dancing thigh

and levitates a bronzed woman
off the seat of her ten-speed bike.
Their bodies bend, loop, twist, and twirl
like winter wheat in a wind storm.

Entranced, they embrace the demon
in the boy drummer's voodoo snare.

III

Debutantes from Anchorage,
the city's blueblood neighborhood,
seem frightened by a sax's wail
and the stench of poverty.

As they bravely tap a Gucci toe,

their faux-fur coats compliment

the booths of garish art and the smiles

painted on each junkie artist's face.

A dobro slides a lean row

of "Voodoo Queen" between

the earthy sound of horns and bass,

plowing toward the Delta from Chicago.

The whole crowd dreams in song,

hypnotized by song as dream.

IV

Before long, I wonder why I'm here,

bland and limp, like politicians

or spaghetti with no sauce, sharing

air burned by the scent of cheap wine

and the hint of antebellum angst

painted on these faces. A girl standing

on my right declares her pregnancy

through meth-stained teeth.

The father plays guitar onstage and wears

23

a hat that reads "Jesus is my boss."
Here's what I've brought to offer back
these souls that give me words,

a tiny bit of my own death,
the exhalation of my breath in strophes.

Catastrophe

Outside the local bank stabbing
litter with a broom-handle and nail spear,
gleaning gum wrappers and cigarette butts
from asphalt like a starving crow in a corn field
the man, oblivious to the possibility
of a fiery demise, turns his blank stare skyward
and the hard blue cracks open his mind.
A series of thoughts—the time
his sister-in-law asked him to make love
and more frightened of her beauty
than his own wife's reaction he failed,
the lottery ticket he forgot to buy
on the day his special number won,
his lack of grandchildren,
wars he did or did not fight, the fact
he never knew why
in autumn leaves change color—
almost have time to bloom
before he snags a smoldering cigarette
and, without thinking, tosses it
into the trash bag that hangs as a deformity
upon his back. Cloaked in a shroud of flames,
choked by the stench of his own charring flesh,
his mind regrets only the current lack of options.

We sit here stranded though we're all
doing our best to deny it...

—from "Visions of Johanna," Bob Dylan, circa 1966

Associations

Beneath the bushes that circle
the Christian Science Reading Room
a woman's compact, mirror broken,
lies open and empty
like a shucked clamshell.
I'm walking my dog and thinking
how one thing leads to another—how
Mary Baker Eddy parlayed
her fear of doctors into a world religion,
how the dog pisses where other dogs do.
Everything feels linked this morning,
 a cosmology that explains
why a useless make-up kit litters
the doorway to a library full
of ineffective information and both
remind me of the best time in my life,
serious laughter and comedic hopes,
all too real when applied to a generation
bent on self-destruction. Oh, you know
exactly what I mean, that era when Quixote
sold Mambrino's helmet for bell bottom jeans
and a nickel bag, when his Sancho Panza
wore no bra under her tie-dyed tee shirt

and draft cards were for lighting Lucky Strikes.

Just last night, my two friends David

and David were trying to convince me

over bottles of red wine that the Sixties

were more than my romantic memory,

more than fashion and pharmaceuticals,

guitar prophets and sex in elevators, but less

than a revolution or the resurrection

of humanity. Today, I'm sober, skeptical

of our recall and all our viewpoints,

wondering if that last best chance

for utopia was the same dream-colored

make-up it's always been, housed

between the chromed shutters of each era's wars

and applied in the broken mirror of history

until it's exhausted, empty, and cast away.

Lunch Time at the Blue River Inn

A Wandering Jew steers through

the wilderness of duct work,

bearing green leaves on a lush journey

over avant-garde art and Betty Davis posters

as the goat of Azaziel once carried sins

into the ancient night—

without knowledge, without desire.

The cook stirs wild rice soup

while a young farmer sits on a stool

and reads a prophecy of calloused

monotony in his own palms.

Porcelain cups string along a counter top,

unstrung pearls, as Jean, the waitress,

pours coffee into them with trembling hands.

"Twenty years ago, I was going to be a dancer,"

she says. Her left eye twitches and she folds

forks and spoons into paper napkins. Soon,

Jean's dreams will echo around a noon crowd,

like rain that splatters overhead on the tin roof,

rolls off, and disappears in an arid, yearning earth.

The Man Who Taught Me Endurance

I knew a postal clerk with one small job—to untie knots

on misdirected parcels. This wizened gnome hunched

over low wooden tables scarred with scissor wounds,

ink tattoos, and stacked high with every twine feasible:

hemp coils, nylon, polyester, and polypropylene

each braided, kneaded, twisted, cross-hatched, and tangled

in absurd shapes, for example dolly knots that hold loads

only while something tugs the other way. The man

undid them all—double eights for climbers, half-hitches

for those that wouldn't bear weight, true lovers

(these overhand knots must be equal to stay locked),

the hangman, a last one applied when none would hold.

Every day from six a.m. till four p.m. for forty years

he battled boredom by dreaming Marie Antoinette

in her last moments while she inhaled the steel and terror

sparking from the grindstone in the courtyard of her palace.

You Can't Write a Poem in a Palm Beach Starbucks

I

Numbed by pure cane sugar and a surf-like

grating of Jaguar tires on the boulevard,

you stare terrified as housewives spill

cellulite from spandex and drag poodles

in diamond collars slowly by. The coffee

tastes like Conrad's *Heart of Darkness*

dark with trilling beasts burned by greed.

Beside the cashier that won't shut up CD's

rise in perky stacks of Dylan and Kenny G

reminding you that synergy is a fiscal term

not a musical one and that buyers, who may

not always be wise, will be comforted at least

in the knowledge that art has become

quantifiable through purchase power.

II

A man reads his Bible while you wait creatively

for an image to grope its way forward from primal

cesspools in your subconscious, something horrific,

33

anything that might dim the constant Florida sun

for a few moments because only contrast makes

language sing—a suicide when the vanilla cream

runs out, a gun battle over the price of a mocha,

or ICE agents dragging out the Guatemalans

washing dishes and trimming tropical ferns

potted on the tiled patio. It doesn't happen.

Instead, a soft breeze sweeps across the page

and carries off all the fresh ideas in paradise.

An Ordinary Man Goes Shopping at Kroger's

"no more to use the sky forever but live with famine and pain a

few short days." —"Hurt Hawks," Robinson Jeffers

Between the basmati rice and the garbanzo beans

an urge for chaos nested in his brain and waited

to hatch a scream. What drove this need

that would embarrass him and frighten shoppers?

Was it the woman who dropped the ketchup bottle

and left the floor bleeding or his own image

in the angled mirrors above the shelves?

Reflection is the mirror's way of dreaming.

Once he dreamed a white tiger in Vietnam, a sign

his whole patrol claimed was only fog until the roar.

From the seafood aisle the stench of fish forced him

to the produce section. Even there, the sweet scent

of overripe kiwis and organic oranges felt tragic

in a feral wake of swarming fruit flies and housewives.

The idea of screaming filled his mind

with inner consistency. He could prove

all that he believed, and believed

all that he could prove. When does the habit

of pretending faith become the habit of faith?

Intoxicated
Trees list left
When they drink the wind

He had a student who wrote haikus and joined the army.

Her favorite poem they read in class was "Hurt Hawks,"

she confessed in an email from Iraq on the same day

shrapnel severed her spinal chord. Her smile among

a group of teens hoping to buy a case of beer

paralyzed his quest for sound. Hushed by memory,

he filled his cart with cottage cheese and frozen dinners.

What is left over
Is carried
In math and in life

A stirring in the ancient sea, where he had come from

nothing and all, where the currents connected him to life

before and after time, almost gave him voice.

The line from a poem took it away.

A Dangerous Thing

My son calls at 3 A.M., enraged
at his impotence—not sexual,
a subject we would never discuss.
Adrenaline fills his voice
as phlegm. A clacking sound
leaking from the next apartment booms
across the phone line as if his neighbor
were a dancer and her head, a broken heel
out of time with a partner's angry rhythms.

"I dialed the cops," he said.
"But, I should do more."
He wants to kick the door down and drag
the boyfriend out by his hair because men
don't beat women. I had taught him that.

What I hadn't mentioned also
was that compassion can be
like compressed air under water,
crucial to human life
but deadly the deeper you dive.
It bubbles in your veins,
intoxicates and liberates your mind

until you lose your sense of caution

in a hostile world and then you drown.

Bee Spring Lodge on Kentucky Lake

In the distance a skiff reels on serrated waves.
Whitecaps lacerate light along the dancing bow.
In a deck chair near the dock, I read a newspaper.
How my planet suffers, swimming drunkenly
into war into smog into crack cartels into self-serving
gods into a relentless spiral toward the end
of what we call time. It's a holiday and empty
autos line the dockside, their owners in rented ships
beyond a cut bank sail west toward a failing sun.
Oak trees ripple above me as green and deep as water.
The metal dock squeals against its moorings
like a huge catfish landed and gasping for breath.
An ice machine gives birth to new cubes
and breaks my reverie as the grill, caked
with last year's suet, ignites. The scent of death
rises skyward from the altar of a world gone mad.

Icons

Fifty years ago no one knew a clown
named Ronald would symbolize a nation
on this my sixty-third birthday.
The stench of hash browns deep fried
in beef tallow, the taste of Egg McMuffins
and the sight of girls with hard nipples
fog my mind. Beneath these golden arches
I remember when everything was new—
'57 Chevy Belairs, angora-wrapped rings,
Louisville Sluggers, dial phones, songs
swirled from vinyl, bottled beer with caps
that pried off, like the case of Falls City
Mike Fitch and I swiped from Carl Humphries'
back porch and drank lukewarm at Lafayette Park,
bicycles resting against a swing set.

One thing leads to another
in a nostalgic mind. Now, I recall how
Mike died from cancer twenty years ago,
how I came to visit during that last week
bearing no gifts but bad coffee from this same place,
offering no wisdom, not even the touch of my hand.

                    Now,

I'm wondering when my own time accelerated

without my notice, when fast food

cooked by teen-aged jesters and record players

in wooden boxes became iconic,

when days became minutes, picking up speed

as if the Holley four-barrel on that '57 Chevy

was infused with jet fuel and the engine of my life

bored and stroked so I might arrive nowhere faster.

Mopping the Past at Midnight in the Old County Jailhouse Museum

The stain from some prisoner's piss

scars the faded tile floor.

Though this jail's been closed for years

his sweat lingers in a swirl of cloth and water,

his face—a pattern hanging like a mug shot

out of focus on the steamed window.

The mop shuffles an empty shadow

as if in chains across a moonlit cell.

Oil from my palms and his mingles

in the cracked wooden handle.

Wind whimpers beyond the doorway,

a voice confessing loneliness.

In this felonious air,

this perfume of ammonia

and wasted possibility,

our breath entwines—guest and ghost.

We are the same sad soul.

We are a rush of blood and stardust

across the black sky, a failed attempt

to climb over the walls that binds us here.

The Same Old Hackneyed Song

He wipes the bar, erasing ashes
from last night's flames. Soon, the thirst
will drive a crowd into his world.
Sick from cravings they can't express,
the lonely will drink, hoping the words
run together into mirth.

His only patron, a pale woman, lights up.
The red glow trembles beneath her nose
in gray fog. She offers him a smoke.
"Quit a year ago," he says, but can't quite say no.

She confesses that her first one came
while hiding in a neighbor boy's tree house
as his mom, wracked by polio, called them
to come eat supper. "She was cooking
from a wheelchair and in a neck brace.
We laughed at her. I let the asshole feel me up."

Almost in tears, she lays her hand on his.
He pulls away as four truckers enter
through the open door. Chairs scratch tile,
Waylon Jennings wails from the jukebox.

Breakfast at Denny's, circa 3 a.m.

Inert in the middle

of sizzle and splash,

I am an audience of one

for the bebop jazz

of thumping sandals,

sliding chairs, flapping

wallets, the cow-bell clang

of a bad bearing

in the solitary ceiling fan,

the rattle of a sports page

and a tickling spoon

across the keyboard of one

nearly empty cup of coffee,

a melody that pauses when

the woman at the next table

chews her unbuttered toast

with her eyes closed.

—Fermata.

A Brief and True British History of Important Events from 1600-2000 C.E. with One Slant Rhyme to Help Relieve the Banality of It All

Oliver Cromwell dies of natural causes
even though he is an unbelievable prick.

Charles the Second exhumes his corpse
and kills it again for metaphorical effect.

A British man, name discreetly withheld,
buys the skull to display in public

for school children until 1957 when
it is reburied. There it remains toxic

to Royalists who will one day dig it up
and rub it in dog shit, a fate that's karmic,

a fact more Indian than English. Or,
so Rupert Murdoch reports.

The English Professor Reflects on Career Choices

"He not busy being born is busy dying." —Bob Dylan

My friend Matthew stuffs dates with goat cheese and bakes
delicacies from countries, their names I can't pronounce.
We are having a party. I laugh, drink gin, and say
to no one in particular, "It doesn't get better that this."
I heard that cliché an hour before I got here. A truck driver
whispered those words to some indifferent waitress
he attempted to impress with an erudite air
and a dollar bill he handed her for some burnt coffee.
Fading into the diesel-driven night, his shadow limped after.

I wonder which of us is more sincere or if irony matters.
We've both spent our lives hauling someone else's freight
over miles of chopped up highways, hopped up on caffeine,
loneliness, and hungry at the wrong times for the wrong things.
When life smells like gasoline and cheap perfume
what does it matter if the road is paved with asphalt or ideas?

Four Hundred Years Before a Professor's Wife Runs Off

When Montaigne discovered cannibals

eat their foes for vengeance rather than taste,

he uncovered the future of divorce.

Today, I saw Donald drunk again

outside his classroom in an indigo shirt listing

left then right, like Blue Sage in a breeze,

his blanched fingers tight on the doorknob

as if his wife leaving had left him too tired to turn it.

I had the urge to catch him though he hadn't fallen

except from grace. Almost Adamic, he gnawed

his own heart, making Montaigne correct.

"It is more barbaric to eat a man alive than dead."

Hos natura modos primum dedit

(This is the first law of nature).

A Matter of Priorities

Why smoke Cohibas when Dutch Masters

are still made? My dad asked me once

in his waning years when constancy meant

everything and appearance meant nothing at all.

Unlike me, he would never have moved to Palm Beach

because palm trees offer no shade and wimps play golf.

He would despise the afternoon Starbucks crowd,

the sham of fruit smoothies and the blithe air

of Birkenstocked shoppers whose souls need Gucci

to fuel their existence. Beneath the braised blue sky

he'd see cops on street corners writing tickets

for BMW's they could never afford to drive,

immigrants in denim coats trimming hedges

that surround homes they will never enter. He would

smell oranges and orchids choked with the sweat and smoke

rising from cane fields and praise the Everglades as it

struggles to drape a fern cape across banks and malls.

He would know, in South Florida raindrops are stars falling.

On Being Lucky Enough to Still Be Alive

Now I know my dad's obsession with waking.
He read the obituaries in the paper first thing
while his wife of fifty years cooked eggs.
"Hurrah! My name's not here," he would cry.

Unlike robins and tulips, roses and squirrels, lions
and pine trees, we don't fully blossom as we die.
Something important gets left undone
and someone important regrets our absence.

It's been easy to grow sad growing old, to fixate
in memoriam on my adolescent love for Denise
and a canary yellow Chevy, to miss the scent
of God in the air while hiking a mountain range

one morning forty years ago in Maine.
With each passing day, faces fade from memory,
warnings hide in a crow's cry, and the weight of time
pins me beneath the shadow of a word I can't speak.

Food for Thought at Dick Clark's Diner

Dick discovered pizza while shooting

craps in Vegas decades ago, his slight

vacation from flipping beef patties

on a hot grill. The cheesy snack

was a free treat for gamblers

at the Rivera, designed to satiate

hunger without breaking their rhythm,

something mobsters brought from Italy

so you could hold, chew, and still shake dice.

At least that's the way the story goes.

Dick flew the concept home to Indiana,

his only winning bet, tomato-sauced

and topped with grease to share locally.

Families flocked to his diner

and ate this big city sensation,

a Sunday special after church.

One hog farmer named Bob Key

built his own—cheddar and pickles

piled on barbequed pork. Today,

forty years later, the Bob Key

is still a monument to clogged arteries,

more popular than the breaded,

deep-fried tenderloin, more deadly

than the foot-long Coney Dog, a way

to remember an icon of the pork industry

who, overcome by methane gas,

fell face down into a pool of hog shit

and drowned. They were close friends,

which may have caused Dick to keep

the menu item in memoriam.

In war there are no unwounded soldiers.

—Jose Narosky

Meditations on the Jungle Ambush

There were nights, strands of time tied together with a thin wire of fear
when you could hear the full moon keening as it rose to wait for death.

Its only job was to end someone's loneliness forever by lighting
the path of a sniper's bullet or casting a dim shadow across a trip wire.

You wanted to believe it hung there to run the tides at China Beach,
guide the course of love you hoped to feel one day, the leap and swirl

of Basa fish or the unlocking of a Cac Dang flower, echo a tiger's growl
or a Black Kite's song, record explosions of dew across the rice paddies.

Everything, even the hard click of brass as a round got chambered,
seemed more romantic and buoyant in the oblique and ductile glow.

In the end, all it did was burnish, and then not even from its own fire,
the monstrous clouds roiling above the banyan canopy overhead.

All it ever did was tempt you with its silent dusting of sugared light
to forget that each night ambush held the origin of your oblivion.

A Veteran Visits the Battlefield at Parker's Crossing, Tennessee

The store is a "middle-of-nowhere" place
stuffed with Confederate flags, toy muskets,
cheap statues of Nathan Bedford Forrest,
and peanut brittle. I've stopped for fuel
at Parker's Crossing because the tank's empty
and to quote my old man on his gambling days—
"This is the only game in town."

My nightmares have always been silent
even on Halloween, but over the pump and flow
of fuel, beneath the cries of flocking crows,
beyond the clicking gallon counter,
and in spite of my wife's incessant chatter,
sounds no longer from this natural world
rise in empty fields behind the building.

If I'm lucky, I'm insane and the sounds
carried on the autumn air are not real.
This explains with less terrifying logic
the moans from a thick-throated wind,
the drum of boots on scarred earth, rifle fire,
the thud of northern steel against the soft flesh

of southern pride and the rush of a current

in the blood-red creek bed dry for a hundred years.
It's all so vivid, as if the wind bridged time,
and the echoes of brother crying over dying brother
were meant to animate my scarred dreams,
as if this simple store was built on blanched bones
and filled with cheap souvenirs to remind me
ghosts are the only true tribute to war.

In Country—1968

When I read this phrase in a Borges poem—

"the desirable dignity of having died"

I thought of my friend, Rick

sitting alone on that sandbag bunker

ten thousand miles from home his final day

in-country. He must have chosen

the cry of the black kite bird,

stench of cordite, sting of blood,

and our last patrol together

beneath the bright blue sky of Hue

over winter in Kansas full of bad whiskey

and the guilt that grows in the soil of solitude

as the best way to end an exceptional life

when he fired that round through his own brain

and eased his dread of leaving the dead behind.

Transubstantiation

My ball cap has faded from Navy blue
to cobalt and finally baby blue. Sculpted
years ago with sweaty hands, it still fits.

As a Catholic, I was taught substance is
what it is within itself. My cap is not my cap
because it is my cap. A little drunk, I think

of this gift from Father Bernie who sipped
wine and ate bread at just the right time
so as to swallow the body of Jesus Christ

and not be a cannibal. The act seems
brilliant in these hours of limbo before night ends
and day arrives. I will eat my cap and swallow

more bourbon until this midnight Eucharist becomes
Rick Sweedeen and Dickie Wolfe, Charlie Schulteis
and Joe Sayyah, Jimmy Hayes and the nameless boy

I shot in Vietnam forty years before tonight
was ever born. From life to death and back to life,
guilt transformed and the past denied by pretense,

this is the mystery my priest shared as he blessed me

into battle for a country I no longer recognize and a god

I never knew. Substance is what something is and I am not.

Visiting the Museum of Hostages, Slovenia, 2003

"Cowards die many times before their deaths. The valiant never

taste of death but once." —*Julius Caesar*, William Shakespeare

In this photograph a young man lingers,

awaiting death like it's the next bus home.

He's bound to a bullet-scarred tree,

his eyes half-closed as if he naps

after having fed on ripe strawberries

from a picnic lunch, as if the blue flame

of sky and a bottle of good Riesling

made him drowsy and content, unaware

of the Nazi pill boxes and trenches I see

that still ring the field with memories of hate.

The guide explains that these silent cell blocks

once locked away a whole town of farmers

and their families. One morning, they were

set free to flee the Russians marching

through the Soca Valley like red ants

devouring all human flesh in their path,

or so the Nazi soldiers told them.

The prisoners ran, blinded by their lust

for liberty more than fear of its reason.

When the fir trees along the hillcrest spread
out before them like pillars from heaven,
machine guns inside the bunkers spat
unrestrained fire. Weeping women fell
like stones and covered children. The men
turned and fought the lead wind with bare hands.
Blood and flesh roiled like wheat chaff in the field.

I asked why this man was tied and shot last.
"He refused to leave his cell; therefore his captors
made him watch his family die first."

Namesake

Uncle Jim owed his sister nothing,
not abstinence from gin or vows
to quit smoking, no three bedroom house
with white picket fence and children
playing hopscotch on the front walk, no
guilt over his impotence. Consequently,
my mom was the only woman he trusted.

One day, a recurring headache
became unbearable. He sought
sanctuary without judgment.
I wish he would have died right there
in our kitchen over dinner.
Life best lived falls off the fast edges.

Six months later the nurse held
a Lucky Strike in his trach tube
to feed the habit. We listened
as the phlegm growled
and watched as the catharsis of cancer
from lung to brain and back again
cured his addiction.

Five packs at 25 cents a pack,

a hundred smokes a day,

the need was all he owned

except for a crinkled photo of Jean,

who divorced him after his two week drunk

        —her honeymoon—

and a pack of "Pinkies" unused condoms

stowed in his wallet "For luck," he said once.

Oh, I guess he owned other things too

if you count dog tags, malaria,

and his insatiable need for booze that grew

from World War II and his time on Iwo Jima

where so much brutal and random death

would puzzle both physicists and theologians.

Even though my uncle seemed like both to me

on frosty morning fishing trips, he was neither

and finally, the weight of memory killed him.

Waterboarding

Today, the neighbor
hosed his garden
in a rainstorm.

His madness nearly
killed the roses.
They panicked.

Fear of drowning
brought each calyx
to the act of surrender.

Petals wilted. My futile friend
reduced his prize possessions
to four bushes full of thorns.

The Moon Walk, July 20, 1969

To follow the moon behind the Legion Hall,

scoop cinders honeycombed by the steam

of locomotives chugging freight through town,

toss them at glass insulators atop the telephone poles

that line the tracks, and hope I might hit one finally

as the holey stones whistle through the vapid air,

this is my wish tonight carried home from Vietnam,

to be a child again, relive Sandy Koufax dreams

out here on Hall's Hill, and crossing the tracks, pierce

the thick woods—oaks, elderberries, pines—behind

Adams Hardware Store, snake through the briar patch

that flowers onto a meadow full of dandelions, to go back

while the world goes forward and cheers strange men

in white suits who, unlike the fallen in every war,

will be born again from a womb of black sky.

There's a Lesson for Us on the Perfume River

Litchi leaves, mangosteens, orchids, and flame trees

all carried on an August breeze are offered to the river

whose name is the fragrance rising from their decay.

The woman's work sings a song ancient and ageless

as her parchment face in honor of the great Perfume.

Beneath the woven roof of bamboo, she lights a fire,

boils her breakfast tea, and then loads a small boat

with baskets of colza, cabbage, fennel, and peppers

grown in fertile soil that bonds her soul to those

who came before and those who will come after.

Her frame, twisted by toil and time, begins to pole

the boat through shallows. Bare feet keep a drum beat

stern to bow and bow to stern a steady rhythm

for the melodies of toucans, black kite birds, and all

the shrill harmonies alive in jungle banyan trees.

With the slow current, she takes this trip to market

while children harvest rice along the river banks,

while the sun spreads like butter on the Purple City.

Her bare feet keep a steady drumbeat bow to stern,

stern to bow while men pull their nets of basa fish

to shore through the four Chinese eras, the defeat

of Kublai Khan, the slavery of the French,

and the slaughter of her children by the Di bo Chet.

Not once in two millennium does she ask her god

about the horror of being and the horror of going on.

In the Butterfly Room at the Chattanooga Zoo

A Monarch settles

       on the wrist of a soldier

deploying soon

          to war.

His wife snaps a photo of the bond

and does not know

       this instant

will be the one that lasts   forever

even if he comes home.

The War Remnants Museum in Ho Chi Minh City

Fenced in by tanks and defused fuel air bombs,

I snap photos of other tourists as they hesitate

to run their timid hands over tools of death.

Why do we hold sacred the refuse of war?

My son asks with innocent curiosity as we

stand before the barrel of a rusted Howitzer

beneath the yellowed palms in Saigon.

It has to do with hope, I tell him, not a violent

awful faith in one god's power over another's

or the belief lottery tickets will cure the disease

driving their purchase, not even the expectation

of immortality, but that history may one day

teach some future, kinder people peace.

Survivor's Guilt

The dog walks with purpose this morning,

leading me precisely somewhere unimportant,

uncaring when each time she returns from chasing

a squirrel that the beast will never be caught.

The street swells with silence as I exorcise

a feeling, which isn't real really, more exhaustion

from nightly dreams and the struggle with daily ones.

I'm okay, the doctors say. In fact, I'm pretty good

in spite of the years spent wrecking this machine

of blood and muscle. If I could stop this obsession

for me by me, I might even be happy instead of startled

when my heart skips a beat, resigned instead of trembling

when I remember one day I'll die and not remember.

The shame and joy that I came home from war alive

festered as one for forty years, an ulcer in my gut,

and here is what I know finally from the pain—

all that I owe must be paid one day soon.

My life will end, not as it should have in youth

when it would have been weightless with fantasy,

but heavy and tedious with truth.

I roll on a wave and look at white clouds.

—Czeslaw Milosz

Sunrise on the Ohio River
November 23, 2009

an elegy for Jack Myers, teacher and friend

In front of me silt and driftwood
clip along driven by the current past buoys
listing in the breeze. Jets grumble overhead.

Veteran's Bridge flexes its girders,
a muscular moaning with the weight of life
as cars and trucks inch their drivers toward work.

Death rises from the water as a mourning fog,
shaping shadows of a city along the water's edge.
Huge husks of empty brick and glass begin

to penetrate the gloom and enter above
a blue womb of sky. Topaz-crowned mallards
rock across waves, davening as if this river

were a temple. Belle of Louisville, revenant of a more
poetic time, steams around the cutbank and disappears,
her captain left as memory in the wake of history.

Restoration

One April morning,

a white bloom flowered

from the rose bush

in my garden.

The calyx offered

the bud with one

petal missing.

Its shape bore a likeness

to Jerry Garcia's hand,

the chording one injured

by axe in childhood,

not as Jesus' face forms

in bowls of oatmeal

or Mary's on a pancake,

more as empty space

to honor Jerry's lost finger

and all the glorious songs

he played without it.

I inhaled the scent

of this centifolia

and thought things not there

create the genius

of absence,

give the missing

a role in the whole.

After all, Bruneschelli

built his dome

before the tools existed,

and Beethoven composed

the Ninth Symphony

in search of sound.

Musicology 101

On the couch

head propped up by the dog-haired pillow,

I'm staring at the ceiling fan as it rotates.

Each blade moves in time

with the focus of Coltrane's tenor sax

around Johnny Hartman's tender voice.

"Say Something Wonderful" and

they do

to me, only I don't care what.

It's early afternoon, the sun spins

through the blinds and drapes webs of light

cross-hatched across the stereo.

The words of the song ride

a musical raft in a feral river

of rhythm, melody floated above

the silt

and gravel of my conscious mind,

away from the dams and locks of sanity

onto a strange and far away shore

where music is nothing and all, where

dragons bloom and roses breathe fire,
where snow melts into stars and tigers
smell like pine trees. This is the place
elephants go to die and angels
renounce their wings. I am an instant
as it burns to ashes and drowns.

Vanishing Point

Children stroke for the line
where water and sky join

to unknown kingdoms, where
greetings come in magic tongues.

Their joys escape in scattered smiles
and their youth, buoyed on transitory tides.

Parents clutch at them as they
struggle on propelled by inner power

born from salt, sea, sun, and purity
of purpose that age will weaken. Even now

it fades as they are hauled finally onto sand
amid the broken conch shells and shadows.

It's time to leave the sunlight, to face a life
without the beach. Meanwhile the brine

beckons always with jade hands
out past the breakers rolling onward

in an irrevocable clash between moon and earth

till wave becomes cloud becomes wave becomes

The Last Member of the Last Congregation at the Barn Abbey in New Harmony Dies

An upright piano, a fireplace, a cross crowned

with thorns, and beneath the cathedral ceiling

a dozen folding chairs once filled with souls

who believed the holy ghost of Pastor Rapp

would pray them into heaven, this is what she sees

while hiking through a gray storm, turning toward

the bay window in the abbey for the last time.

Her glance into the glass, more curious than reverent,

reflects her coat graced by rivulets of purple rain.

Her eyes blink, flecked with revenants of the flock

she follows past the tiny church into the graveyard.

Across the bottom land beyond, the Wabash

winds its way around the bend. Drifting on,

the river stays in place, a paradox as confused

as the current of faith that carries her from death

to endless life below a marble stone where

she will disappear and remain forever.

The Beachcombing Poet

for Volha

Denim sky fades to gray
as dawn jumps the breakers.
Her feet shuffle over shadows of starfish,
ancient shells, and ghosts from primal eras.
Her mind trolls one wave and then more.
Like the nettles swimming in the bay
driven by hunger toward some prey's
intoxicating death, her thoughts spin
with the poison of words, sting
rhythms, and bind them tightly
in tentacles of translucent strophes.
This is the need that drives her forward
into the blinding surf to taste the salt
and copper on her lips, to feed
the source and rot of her own cells
and swallow what lies beneath the waves.

Capitalism

Outside my sister's country home five wild turkeys
stretch worms out of black dirt, strut, and flex their wings
as if the sky might suddenly free them from its gray weight.

A doe and two fawns graze on the patchy grass of spring,
nudge the birds aside to search for more, and freeze in place.
I think the squawks and flutters have alarmed the deer,

caused them to rethink their actions, but I can't be sure.
No sound echoes through the bay window. The kitchen,
like space, is a vacuum, separating me from the world.

Then, it comes, a buzz saw with legs and teeth,
seething drool and hackled backs, a pack of wild dogs
with no regard for harmony, only personal hunger

and the need to feed that has fermented in their bellies
from a time beyond time, a prehistoric urge that separates
beasts from mere animals and proves evolution has its limits.

In an instant, the deer have fled, the dogs have savaged
two turkeys beneath a copse of oaks and maples.
The rest, a gaggle of feathers and fear, beat the air senseless

until, unable to rise above the chaos, they ignore it
and return to their harried search for earthworms.
Forgetting has purified their souls.

Breakfast at Denny's—A Different Morning

If you could comfort any person

who chokes down a Grand Slam breakfast,

it would be the man in the Boy Scout shirt.

Coffee in hand, his rheumy eyes stare

at the reflection in the glass window.

It's not the filthy blond disheveled hair,

the twisted lips and purple gums or chewed

fingernails that scrape his scarred chin,

not the torn boots or crusted khaki pants

worn to a final sheen that drive you

to an opposing wall so much as the stench

rising from his soul and the talk he's having

with his own insane image. You want to help

but won't come close enough to hear the words

for fear they might infect you with his disease.

Somewhere, hidden deep in everyone,

there's a memory that will destroy dreams.

Not Much Happens Sitting
in a Parked Car Waiting for Erin

The first drops of rain freckle the windshield,

but patterns elude me no matter where I search.

Not just the obvious images—Orion, the face of Jesus,

the dog's favorite toy, a state ridden through in childhood—

are absent. Even pretend lines drawn with purpose

between the wet spots disappear into madness

beyond the glass where a drunk mutters how

he'll bitch slap his shadow if it keeps chasing him,

where tourists snap photos of oak trees that seem

less boring on Frankfort Avenue than their country farms

and small town gravel roads, where the Mexican boy

sweeps the sidewalk with the same motion

he swung a sickle on some dusty hillside near Juarez,

where the sky thunders and the scent of ozone

clings to hickory smoke and honeysuckle, where

the train whistle rattles a cyclist who pedals by,

where chaos evolves from design, where the earth spins
and returns to the same place it has never been.

The (Brief) History of Poetry

So, for me this poem thing kicked off
with Enheduanna, high priestess of Ur
who, four thousand years before
Shakespeare fancied his first sonnet,
laid language in the open arms of love,
caressed it till Sappho sexed up Homer's
wine dark sea that the waves might bear
Shelley, Keats and Blake to shore where
rhyme languished till Eliot and Pound
blew smoke up its ass and triggered
an addiction to substance over form.
Now, coughing phlegm and lighting Kools,
subject to seizures and bad breath, my words
drink bourbon unrestrained in some seedy
backwater Bukowski kind of bar awaiting
new Strophes that may never show
or, even if they do, buy another round.

Polemics

Here's a mistake I frequently make,
I say poems are made from words.
But that is to say killing is an ordinary
task in war or all the tools for every job
come from Sears. Tonight, my poem
works as a bartender who, like an acrobat,
leaps on a narrow shelf. Steadied
by one leg and a waitress
with arms covered in pagan tattoos,
he retrieves a bottle high
above the bar's mirror breaking
neither neck nor sweat. Tonight
my poem is love as these two people
brush against each other and hesitate
till all that needs said is said in silence.
Leaves fall from trees outside
without fearing death. The bartender
doesn't know this. That must be why,
drying glasses with a damp towel,
he trembles each time she returns.

From My Front Porch

Across the street:

A blue chair leans against the dumpster,

exhausted by the look of its faded cover.

With a leftward list, missing buttons

and seams shredded, death is its inevitable

outcome from entertaining assholes daily.

Think how anger damaged the heart

each time some overweight half-drunk

family breadwinner plopped down,

white-knuckled grip on a can of Bud,

and farted. Think how tears destroyed

its emotional balance as the wife curled

her legs across the sad fabric and read

romance novels, or how disgust drove

the poor thing to a trash heap after Junior

masturbated in the cushions watching porno.

Still, an air of dignity lingers visibly

in its erect bearing and lack of complaint.

II

Our Semi-Successful Garden:

Oh sophisticate, urbanite tree-dweller,

Oh, hairy John Robie, Alfred Hitchcock

would be proud of the irony as you

scurry up a telephone pole parked

next to my old Lincoln with another

of my wife's red jewels clutched

in your jaws. As you chew and savor

the pulp, she who must be obeyed

will spit and sputter, berating my sloth

for not protecting her tomatoes from

"the same fucking squirrel

that stole them all last summer."

Then, winter will come.

Next summer you will reappear,

barring unforeseen Goodyear tire tracks

across your furry back, and pluck

my soul as it sprouts along the wilting vine.

Why did you choose this garden in a whole

city full of pretend farmers who cultivate

their 12 foot by 12 foot produce patch

with more diligence than me? Do the weeds

make me seem more user-friendly,

or is it the russet leaves that should be green?

III

My neighborhood:

The Blue Healer herds her as if she were

a calf straying toward the curb—

girl and dog on a relentless trek

to the bagel shop down the block, drawn

this dawn by the scent of baking bread.

Around me bird song crinkles

like leather soles dancing over broken glass,

the tip tap of white canes signal

a class in session around the corner

at the School for the Blind, and across the alley

yoga gurus on rubber mats face outward

toward oncoming traffic, hoping to stall

the passage of time with their ceramic gaze.

I taste the last sip of lukewarm coffee

as if it were my Eucharist to lethargy

and realize the only Holy thing

worthy of my worship is Stevie Nicks.

IV

My Utilitarian Outlook:

Dew dusts the parked cars and pastes

a few dead leaves to the damp concrete.

Someone named Heidi sticks a "for sale" sign

on the front lawn next door, reminding me

that my own landlord seems unable

to motivate the landscaper. I know this

because the gas company sent me notice

last week—an untrimmed knot of weeds

has rendered the meter unreadable; therefore

an estimate will have to be made.

I translate said message into English,

"We can now fuck you legally."

An ambulance screams along Frankfort Avenue,

its shadow followed by the sun and loneliness.

V

The Homeless Man:

Jesse James sleeps in Bingham Park

on a bench next to the merry-go-round.

Bob Howard killed the wrong cowboy.

Covered in cast-off western wear,

sporting string tie and buckin' bronc

belt buckle, he tips a twisted Stetson

my way on his daily walk by as if to say

"being from Kentucky you know why

I married my cousin Frieda

and choose to live alone."

Shuffling on, his scuffed boots stumble
over cracks in the concrete walk
as he unfurls a large red umbrella
that protects his dying way of life
from the ghosts of falling stars.

                    VI

Definitions:

In my younger days the bridge between truth
and fiction was built by urgent hunger
like an ice cream headache, and not memory.
This city block was filled with children
who pushed swings so high they all giggled
from fear, who rode red bikes with baskets
and whitewall tires, who played Whiffle ball
in backyards and pitched like Sandy Koufax
and hit like Hank Aaron, if only in their dreams.
The girls screamed at garter snakes in gardens,
followed their freckled footsteps playing hopscotch,
jumped rope until they learned of gender roles
and explored their bodies with joy and shame.
Always, the grass grew only in patches,
like a boy's beard, over the clay cheeks of earth.
Sunlight tickled like butterfly wings brushed
across a forearm. The scent of clover piggy-backed

on wisps of smoke as mesquite smoldered in the grills.
Fresh paint and bleach shed winter's scarred skin
from every house along the street on April weekends.
The calyx of life bloomed from perennial tombs
and whispered lies of immortality.

VII

Heart:

Doctors call it muscle, a pump primed with blood.
The lonely fill it, like a jug, with unrequited love.
When race horses refuse to quit and run on
beyond the limit of their spindly legs, jockeys brag,
"That horse sure had a lot of heart."
But heart is a small woman, bent double with age
and blind. Each morning she shuffles past my house,
her cane clicking on the cement sidewalk,
and searches for the curb on Frankfurt Avenue.
As she leans against the autumn chill, her nose crinkles
at the warm scent of toasted bagels seeping from a deli.
I have no idea where she goes or how she knows
the traffic light just changed from red to green,
only that she'll make the same trip tomorrow while I
sit here terrified at every step as she crosses traffic.

VIII

True Love:

My neighbor's daughter
and her first boyfriend skip
cracks in the sidewalk,
hold hands and stare
at a Snickers wrapper as it blows
across their blue sneakers.
Above them two squirrels salsa
on a telephone wire and shake
the scent of lilacs from the air.
The boy's lips flutter across hers,
butterfly meets flower petal.
They turn, see me framed
in the window and blush.
I blush back
and wish for a camera
that crystallizes moments,
holds the ineluctable pangs
of hunger forever entwined
with their fingers, that captures
cold sweat in his voice,
and desire on the edge of her fear.

The Birth of Knowledge

Once, I lived in a secret place where
every need was fulfilled before I asked,

where life cuddled me in its fluid arms
and I neither shopped for food nor paid rent,

where sleep came uninterrupted
by bed bug or bad dream, and pain from

the friction of worn-out joints and memories
remained a distant, though inevitable, prospect.

But, there was only darkness there, a liquid
realm of grope and stutter I soon outgrew,

learned to fear instead of honor, a refuge
I ripped and shredded, bled with intent to destroy,

a dimness I detested more
with each peristaltic push toward the light.

Something's Fishy on the Ohio River

In this world where we invent our own delusions

the morning news headline "Many Eating River Fish"

shouldn't bother me in any dietary way, especially

as I enjoy thick sausage gravy and white flour

biscuits at Barbara Lee's Southern Kitchen.

But somehow, the fact that thousands of sentient

beings ate thirteen million pounds of deep-fried

bottom feeder fish for their health from a river

flowing with PCB's strikes me as an odd use of logic.

I suppose the reasoning would seem to some as a sort

of contrapuntal comment on life, a counterpoint harmony

between heart disease and cancer. By courting both

each is cancelled. That makes sense when I bear in mind

my friend Jeff's grandpa smoked unfiltered Camels,

ate double cheeseburgers daily during his ninety-three years,

and always said, "The last best reason for living is irony."

Kick Me, Please

My brother lies in a maze of tubes and wires,

gutted like a salmon by the surgeon yesterday,

victim of ritual designed to stop time.

It seems he won't wake up,

won't breathe unless a machine makes him.

Swollen everywhere, his proximity to death

frightens me. I'm afraid we've left a world

undone between us. We grew distant trying

to survive separate lives we never chose.

Busy mending memories of wars and misfired

relationships, I never told him how sorry I was

that his wife strayed or that he lost his only good job.

Oh, I made some misplaced attempts to reconcile,

like a dog that pisses on the rug and later scratches

at the door. I'd like to think we fought over love

or some great trauma wedged our lives apart.

But, empty greetings at annual family meetings

simply mirrored the slow drift of our unmoored lives.

As a child, I destroyed his favorite toy, a rattle,

to see the mystery inside that caused his laughter.

All I found was sand.

A Sonnet in Honor of Stephen Dobyns' Faded Coat

The denim jacket drips off shoulders rounded,

not slumped, but sculpted on a wheel of words

by the constant file of time. Worn into a second

skin, living tissue, faded blue, creased by friction,

cotton twill surrounds the substance of his genius,

which is not to conclude he wraps it turban-like

or buttons it over his brain to contain his beast.

Rather, it is to reason that a poem's heart attaches

to any sturdy fabric stone-washed by hand, woven

with passion stored along the edge of life, to think

language made meaningful by what warms a man's

blood and through heat assures survival of his soul.

Adventure

The end came quickly
at Jimmy Coomer's birthday party.
After cake and blind man's bluff
I stole his new cork gun, jumped
his tricycle, and pedaled hard
away from cries of flustered guests.

When the sidewalk disappeared
I dropped over the concrete curb.
Gun in hand became gun in mouth,
and teeth scattered, smashed by a law
of physics I wouldn't even hear about
for twelve more years and never grasp.

The next two hours tasted like ether
and stank like hot copper as my father
held me down and old Doc Boren
wrestled jagged remnants of a front tooth
from the pool of blood and tears between
my lip and gums. I have stolen no more

wheeled vehicles these past decades
but a gap remains between my teeth

to spit through or fit a nipple into.

I take this reminder as proof that life

most enjoyed breeds damage, and scars

map the path of my soul more than dreams.

Epilogue

My Childhood Is Dead—Long Live My Childhood

"Time's sovereign. It rides the backs of names cut into marble. And
to get Back, one must descend, as if into a mass grave."
—Larry Levis, "Caravaggio: Swirl and Vortex"

On cloying winter weekends when school was closed
mom bundled me against a wind so hostile to the skin
red cheeks burned as if scratched by a thousand thorns.
She sent me out to play with all the neighbor kids
while she laundered, scrubbed, and baked, as did each
neighbor mom. Dad spent his time away from work
working in the garage, working on the snow-filled
black and white TV, or working with the lawn, as did
each neighbor dad who lived the American dream.
Old Ike had promised every white family that TV,
along with two cars, a picket fence, low mortgage rates,
processed food, dial phones, and a prosperous peace.

The movie house offered Saturday matinees,
the incense of freedom and the shelter of fantasy.

Here, I congregated with grade school friends.

Bug-eyed in 3-D glasses and screaming, we warmed

our blood dodging arrows and Indian ponies that rode

across the plains, out of the screen, and over our heads.

The pasty face of Tom Mix, his Stetson as white

as his face, his six guns blazing and Indians falling,

taught us the color of goodness. The sweet tang

from Dum-Dum suckers distracted us long enough

not to question the old usher, wig askew, who

forced black kids to a secret place called "balcony."

Fifty years have passed since I first stuck a piece

of Wrigley's Spearmint to the bottom of a seat

to kiss a girl named Pam while Elmer Fudd stuttered

through my self-conscious pubescence. Once,

some businessman partitioned the main floor

into four separate screens without vision of a future

where memory and imagination, fractious brothers

that they are, might play, free in a world full

of cell phones and iPads outside the doors.

Now, I'm driving past the movie house one last time.

The marquee's busted, the doors are sealed with plywood,

but the scent of popcorn rushes in the car's open window.

CPSIA information can be obtained at www.ICGtesting.com
Printed in the USA
LVOW040657211112

308100LV00003B/100/P